AMAZING BIBLE MYSTERIES
Incredible but True Stories

Copyright © 1996 Lion Publishing

First published in the United States of America in 1996 by Thomas Nelson, Inc.,
Publishers, Nashville, Tennessee, and distributed in Canada by Word
Communications, Ltd., Richmond, British Columbia.

Text by John Drane

Published by
Lion Publishing plc
Sandy Lane West, Oxford, England
ISBN 0-7459-2180-9
Albatross Books Pty Ltd
PO Box 320, Sutherland, NSW 2232, Australia
ISBN 0-7324-0550 5

First edition 1995
10 9 8 7 6 5 4 3 2 1 0

Contributors to this volume
John Drane is Director of the Center for the Study of Christianity and
Contemporary Society at the University of Stirling and the author of several
highly acclaimed books on the Bible and its background. In this book he presents
the Bible and its history in a way that young people can understand and enjoy.

Alan Millard, Rankin Professor of Hebrew and Ancient Semitic Languages at
Liverpool University, is the consultant for the illustrations in this book, and all
the books in the series.

Acknowledgments
All photographs are copyright © Lion Publishing, except the following:
Ancient Art and Architecture collection: 13
Trustees of the British Museum: 3 (right)
Susanna Burton: 15 (left)
Robert Harding: 1 (below left, middle), 3 (above and below left)
N Hepper: 11
Hulton Deutsch Collection: 10 (right)
The Israel Museum, Jerusalem: 2 (right)
Alan Millard: 2 (left)
Oxford Scientific Films: Wendy Shattil/Bob Rozinski: 7 (right);
P J Devries: 10 (right); Mike Linley: 12; Mike Hill: 18 (right)
N Poulton: 10 (below left), 20 (left)
Z Radovan, Jerusalem: 1 (right), 4 (left)
Lois Rock, courtesy of the Biblical Resources Pilgrim Centre, Tantur: 16 (above)
Zefa: 17, 20 (right)

The following Lion Publishing photographs appear by courtesy of:
Trustees of the British Museum: 8 (right), 19
Israel Museum, Jerusalem: 8 (left)
John Williams Studios: 15 (right)

Illustrations, copyright © Lion Publishing, by:
Chris Molan: 1, 2, 3, 4, 5, 6, 7, 8, 9, 10, 11, 12, 13, 14, 15, 16, 17, 18, 19, 20

Maps and diagrams, copyright © Lion Publishing, by:
Oxford Illustrators Ltd: 1, 2

Bible quotations are taken from the *Good News Bible*, copyright © American
Bible Society, New York, 1966, 1971, and 4th edition 1976, published by the Bible
Societies/HarperCollins, with permission.

Story text is based on material from *The Lion Children's Bible*, by Pat Alexander

ISBN 0-7852-7909-1

Printed and bound in Malaysia

AMAZING BIBLE MYSTERIES

INCREDIBLE BUT TRUE STORIES

John Drane
Illustrations by Chris Molan

THOMAS NELSON PUBLISHERS
Nashville • Atlanta • London • Vancouver

Contents

Page 7

Page 1

Page 1

Page 5

Page 8

Page 4

Page 10

Page 1

Page 2

Page 1

Page 8

1 History and Mystery

Many people claim that the Bible is very special. They find it exciting and challenging to read. But at times, the Bible can seem rather puzzling. Some of the things that happen seem very unlikely!

These things are mysterious in the sense of being "supernatural"— beyond this world. God is described as being central to everything that happens. There is talk of a devil, angels, demons, and so on.

Some of the events that happen in the world of people are quite out of the ordinary, too, even miraculous. Sometimes nature itself seems to be behaving differently from what anyone would expect—dramatic and sudden weather changes, for example. Other times, it seems that certain people can heal those who are sick with a touch, or even bring them back to life.

With stories like these, it is no great surprise that some people begin to wonder if the Bible isn't just made up.

History

At the same time, most of the Bible stories are clearly set in a particular time and place in history. The most recent events happened in the eastern part of the Roman Empire, nearly 2,000 years ago.

Others go back more than a thousand years earlier. They, too, take place in the Middle East— mainly in the countries known today as Iraq, Syria, Israel, Palestine, and Egypt.

Archaeologists have discovered enough evidence from the past to say quite clearly that many of the Bible events are rooted in real history.

Clues to the past

Some remains from Bible times are easy to see. The pyramids stand tall in the deserts of Egypt. Modern Iraq is home to the impressive ruins of ancient Babylon. Every day, thousands of people flock to the one remaining wall of the ancient Jewish temple in Jerusalem.

Other remains fell to the ground long ago and gradually became buried in the soil. Sometimes they are rediscovered by accident. More often, they are unearthed by archaeologists patiently sifting through mounds of rubble at the sites of ancient towns and cities.

◀ The Bible lands
The names of the countries have changed over time. These are the names used today.

◀ Jerusalem
This part of the Jewish temple in Jerusalem has lasted since Jesus' day.

▶ Babylon
Part of a wall from ancient Babylon in present-day Iraq.

▶ Egypt
The pyramids are a reminder of the splendor of ancient Egypt.

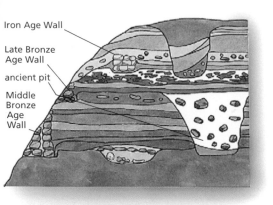

▲ Layers of history
Each layer of rubble dates from a different time.

▼ History in the making
Here are people from Bible times rebuilding their city after a crushing defeat in war. The new city is built on the rubble of the old—burying a good deal of evidence of everyday life before the battle.

In the diagram labels:
Iron Age Wall
Late Bronze Age Wall
ancient pit
Middle Bronze Age Wall

Slicing the history cake

In Old Testament times (the first part of Bible history) the two most important nations in the Middle East were based in Egypt and Mesopotamia. The land where the people of Israel made their home was in between, and the superpowers never stopped fighting for it.

The settlements there were destroyed time and again by well-equipped armies. Once the armies had moved on, the people would construct new homes and workplaces. Each new settlement was built on top of the flattened remains of what had been there before.

Some towns that were first built on flat land were eventually being rebuilt on a high mound! If you could slice through the mounds as you slice through a cake, you would see many layers of rubble spread out, one on top of the other. Each layer contains the remains of the settlement from a different time in history.

These mounds are often referred to by the Arabic word for a mound—a *tell*.

▲ Archaeology in action
In theory archaeologists could uncover a whole mound, or tell, layer by layer. But that would take too much time—and money. Instead, they take a sample slice. Sometimes the finds are very exciting. Archaeologists are careful to photograph everything exactly where it is found before labeling it and taking it away for more detailed study.

 Did you know?
Archaeologists do a lot of research before starting to dig, but they can't be sure they have chosen the right spot.

In 1928 an archaeologist named John Garstang excavated a slice of the remains of a settlement called Hazor, in northern Israel. He found nothing from the period 1400–1200 B.C. and decided that no one had lived there at that time.

Thirty years later, an archaeologist named Yigael Yadin dug into the same mound but took a different slice. He found many remains dating back to those years!

2 A Slice of Life

Most archaeological finds are bits and pieces from the everyday life of ordinary people. From these fragments, people today can begin to work out what everyday life was like in Bible times: the kinds of objects they had in their homes, the kinds of things they used in the work they did, the kinds of toys children played with, and so on.

The people who lived these ordinary lives in the land of Israel are the nation whose story is told in the Bible. Knowing about their story from another angle helps people understand the Bible story better.

▲ Ancient lamp
Simple oil lamps were designed to hold a burning wick in the spout. The rest of the wick trailed in a pool of oil in the center.

Ordinary people used lamps like these in their homes in Old Testament times. It is the kind of lamp they would have thought of when they heard this line from one of the Bible's psalms:

> *Your word is a lamp to guide me and a light for my path.*

▶Synagogue ruins
These ruins are of a synagogue in Gamla, in the region of Galilee.

Jesus sometimes spoke to people in the synagogues of Galilee. Imagine sitting with the children on a stone bench in a small synagogue like this . . . and hearing Jesus talk about stories from the Old Testament, or even seeing Him heal a sick person . . .

Did you know?

From the earliest times, Christians and Jews made regular pilgrimages to the Middle East to visit places mentioned in the Bible. But it was not until the French emperor Napoleon visited Egypt in the eighteenth century that people became really interested in digging up the past.

The nineteenth century was a golden era for archaeology in the region. But still today, more and more finds are being made.

Potted history

Archaeologists always find more pottery than anything else. The reason is simple: Everybody used pots for cooking and eating, and they needed a good supply because pots break quite easily. However, pottery is difficult to destroy completely.

At the end of the nineteenth century, an archaeologist named William Flinders Petrie thought hard about the different styles of pottery that had been found. He reasoned that if the same styles of pottery turned up at different sites, then the layers of rubble in which they were found must all date from about the same time. He hit on the idea of using pottery styles as a way of dating things.

Later research proved him right, and his "ceramic index" is still used by archaeologists today.

Middle Bronze Age   Late Bronze Age

Iron Age   Roman period

◀ **Old Testament jugs**
These jugs or pitchers date from different periods. The first three belong to Old Testament times. The Roman period is the setting for the New Testament.

▲ **Sandals**
Leather sandals from New Testament times, found at the desert fortress of Masada.

The New Testament character known as John the Baptist once saw Jesus coming to visit him and recognized that Jesus was Someone special. He said of Jesus, "I am not good enough even to carry his sandals."

3 Landmark Events

How can people make sure that a great event is remembered for hundreds of years?

One way is to put up a monument or even a building, with words—and perhaps pictures—carved in stone. Such monuments stand out as landmarks in the places where they are built. Neither they nor the events recorded on them can easily be overlooked.

Written details

The written inscriptions on such monuments provide very important information about the event.

A problem arises if the language has been forgotten and no one can read the words anymore. When Western explorers first began looking at the buildings and monuments of Bible lands, they found inscriptions in languages that no one had either written or spoken for many centuries. Experts were baffled by them until one day an officer in Napoleon's army discovered a stone with writing in three languages. One was in Greek, and the others were forms of ancient Egyptian.

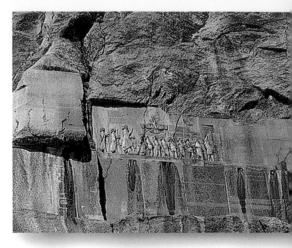

▲ Decoding the cliff writing
This cliff face at Behistun has been carved with an inscription in three ancient languages. It provided the clue for decoding the languages of ancient Mesopotamia.

◄ Three languages
This inscription in three languages provided a vital key to understanding ancient inscriptions. It is called the Rosetta stone.

Jean-François Champollion was a scholar who knew Greek, and from that he managed to work out how the other two languages worked.

His success encouraged others to tackle the languages found in ancient Mesopotamia. One important find was at Behistun, where the Persian emperor Darius I had inscriptions carved into the rock face in three languages—Old Persian, Babylonian, and Elamite. By comparing these, scholars were able to make sense of them.

By the middle of the nineteenth century archaeologists were able to read most of the inscriptions they were finding.

The Bible in history

A number of ancient monuments and inscriptions record events mentioned in the Bible from the point of view of other nations, but that still match with events as told in the Bible. These finds clearly show that the Bible contains books of real history.

Matching stories

In 701 B.C., King Sennacherib of Assyria invaded Judah and defeated many towns. People today can find out about the story from two sides:

The Judean story
A verse from the Bible states:

"In the fourteenth year that Hezekiah was king of Judah, Sennacherib, the emperor of Assyria, attacked the fortified cities of Judah and captured them. Then he ordered his chief official to go from Lachish to Jerusalem with a large military force to demand that King Hezekiah surrender."

▲ **The Assyrian story**
King Sennacherib of Assyria had a room of his palace decorated with pictures of his victory over the Judean city called Lachish.

This portion shows Sennacherib on his throne. The cuneiform inscription (of which you can see a part in the top left of this picture) reads as follows:

"Sennacherib, king of the world, king of Assyria, sat on a seat and the booty of Lachish passed before him."

4 The Book of the Faith

Archaeology shows that Bible history is written about events that really happened. The Bible itself is a document that dates back a very long time.

Copies of copies

The original documents written by the Bible's authors all disappeared long ago. Even the oldest manuscripts of the Bible known today are copies of copies. But there are so many thousands of them that more is known about the Bible than any other ancient book.

What the Bible says—especially what it says about God and God's relationship with people—is something that has been treated as serious and worthy of respect for a very long time indeed.

Ancient books compared

Copies of part of the Hebrew Bible go back to about 400 B.C. Several complete Christian Bibles (including both Old and New Testaments) were copied between 200 and 300 C.E. There are also thousands of odd sheets and pages from even earlier dates.

This contrasts with other ancient works of literature that are also respected as important documents. For example, a Greek historian named Thucydides wrote between 460 and 400 B.C., but today fewer than ten very old copies of his work are left—and the oldest of them was written in 900 C.E.!

A Roman historian named Tacitus wrote at the end of the first century C.E., and only two manuscripts of his work survive. One is from the ninth century C.E. and the other from the eleventh century.

The Dead Sea Scrolls

One of the most astonishing discoveries of ancient Bible texts took place in 1947.

In the spring of that year, a herdsman named Jum'a Muhammed was looking after goats near the Dead Sea. He was throwing stones at the cliff face to amuse himself. One went in a cave, and he heard the sound of breaking pottery.

His cousins went inside, and found his stone had broken a large jar, containing a leather roll with ancient writing on it.

There were many jars in other caves, over 400 rolls in all.

The scrolls had been put there by members of a Jewish religious community at nearby Qumran. They wanted to protect their valuable library when the region was in turmoil as Roman armies fought against Jewish guerrillas in about 68 C.E.

Some scrolls give information about the way of life of the community. But most are books of the Hebrew Bible, and the oldest had been written in Old Testament times.

►**Scribes at Qumran by the Dead Sea**
An imaginary scene in the writing room (scriptorium) of the community buildings at Qumran shortly after the time of Jesus. Writing is being laid aside so members of the community can get on with the urgent work of taking their library of scrolls to hiding places in the many small caves in the surrounding cliffs. In their determination to save their precious Scriptures from the Romans, these Jewish people actually saved them for nearly 2,000 years—and today the remains are carefully looked after in a museum in Jerusalem.

►**Safe hiding**
Inside one of the caves in the cliff face where the scribes from Qumran hid their scrolls. Thousands of fragments have been found here.

Ancient manuscripts

In 1839, the German Constantin von Tischendorf was a young man of twenty-four. He was fascinated by the Bible, and was determined to discover as much as he could about its history.

He found some old manuscripts that had lain unnoticed for centuries in the famous libraries of Europe. But he believed the oldest of all must be in the Bible lands themselves.

He visited an ancient Christian community at the foot of Mount Sinai in May 1844: St. Catherine's Monastery. Here he found what he was looking for—the most ancient manuscript he had ever seen, containing the complete New Testament and much of the Old Testament as well. Unfortunately, the monks had no idea of its value and were burning it in the library furnace. Tischendorf persuaded them not to destroy any more of it, but it was fifteen years before they agreed to give it as a gift to Tsar Alexander II of Russia.

It became known as Codex Sinaiticus. A codex is the old name for a book of pages rather than a scroll, and Sinaiticus refers to Mount Sinai where it was preserved.

It is a copy made in the fourth century C.E., and is still the most complete ancient Bible manuscript known to exist.

Tischendorf commented: "I would rather have discovered this manuscript than the crown jewels of the Queen of England." It was—and is—a treasure of immense value.

▲ **Monastery**
St. Catherine's Monastery at Mount Sinai where a very old copy of the Bible was found

▲ **Codex Sinaiticus**
A close-up of a page of the ancient Bible, the Codex Sinaiticus

5 Mysteries Beyond Time

Studying the archaeology of the ancient Near East and poring over the oldest Bible manuscripts help people see how the Bible and its people fit into history. But Christians do not treasure the Bible because it is a window to times past but because they believe it is a window to God. In its many different types of writing they find ways of understanding mysteries beyond time itself.

Mysterious questions

Many things about this world are hard to understand. Where did everything that exists come from? Why are there so many different races of people in the world? Why do bad things happen to good people? Does life make sense, or is it just a jumble of different things that no one can explain?

There are no easy answers to such questions. Neither science nor history can answer them. Because they are so difficult to answer, people have long told stories in an effort to understand them.

A story from beyond time

Long before the Bible was written, the people of Mesopotamia had their own stories of how the world began. One of them was an old Akkadian tale, almost ninety lines long and written on seven clay tablets in cuneiform script.

It is known as *Enuma Elish*, from the words with which it begins and that mean "When on high." Like the Bible story of creation, it is written in poetry. And it begins in a similar way:

When on high the heaven had not yet been named,
And below the firm ground had not yet been
given a name...

As the story unfolds, it tells how Apsu and Tiamat—the ocean and the life-giver—created a number of gods, who then revolted against them. Apsu the ocean was killed by a magic spell, and Tiamat the life-giver determined to get her revenge. In the battle that followed, she was killed by the god Marduk, who divided her body in two, to make heaven and earth.

Later, people were made from the blood of one of Tiamat's allies—Kingu. Their purpose was to do all the everyday jobs for the gods.

The story asks why life is often violent and unfair, and why people never seem to be able to change things. Its answer is that this is how the gods intended it to be. When people are violent, they are just behaving like the gods.

▼ **A foreign festival**
At one time, the Jewish people lived in Babylon and saw for themselves the New Year Festival celebrating the Akkadian creation story. Undaunted, many Jewish families passed on their own story about God making the world, and God's love for it.

Another story—another view of the world

At the time the Hebrew Bible was written many people knew the Akkadian tale of creation. It was reenacted every year in Babylon at the New Year Festival. But the Jewish people had long experience of seeing God working in their own lives and the life of their nation. That experience told them that God was different.

They had their own stories, which use the same kind of picture language that is found in *Enuma Elish,* but describe a different view of the world and how everything works.

They believed the world is in the hands of a loving and caring God, who is always on the side of right. The Bible always describes the natural world as a good place for people to live.

People have an important place in this good world. They are not created to serve gods who are cruel and unpredictable. On the contrary, both women and men are made "in God's image": Their purpose is to reflect what God is like and for that reason they find happiness in being loving and caring—as God is.

They are not forced to reflect God's love. As a result, there are bad things in the world. But people can work to mend them, to work for peace and justice.

6 A God of Love and Justice

The Bible begins with stories told in response to life's big questions. The first page imagines a time before anything at all existed—except for God.

A life-giving God

Then God started to have fun, making light and darkness, lots of wonderful colors, fields and forests, oceans and mountains—and people.

No one knows exactly when this story was written, nor how the people of ancient Israel used it. But it is a poem, and might easily have been a song to celebrate all the good things of this world.

It has a refrain that is repeated six times: "God saw that it was good." This message is one of the most important things the Bible has to say about God. God likes this world, and He is on the side of everything that is good. God cares about the environment, and all the living things on this planet. God is on the side of life, and He wants people to enjoy it to the full.

▲ **God's wonderful world**
The Bible says that God made everything in the world and that it was good—full of beauty and fun.

▼ **Jesus shows God's love**
Christians believe that Jesus shows them what God is like. Jesus welcomed people—children and grown-ups, poor and wealthy, wrongdoers and respectable religious types. He said God does the same.

A God of justice

The Bible tells many stories about all kinds of people. Because they all deal with the life of one nation—the people of Israel—it can be seen as one long story. Throughout, one thing never changes: God is always on the side of justice.

The laws of the Old Testament tell people to give special care to those who suffer and are mistreated. For example, they required farmers to leave the edges of their fields unharvested, so that the poor could help themselves and have food without having to buy it. The laws also gave special protection to groups such as widows, orphans, and foreigners, who often had a hard time.

The reason for all this was simple. At the beginning of their national history, the people of Israel had been enslaved by a cruel king in Egypt. There seemed no possible way of escape—until God stepped in. In the face of great injustice, God inspired Moses to face up to the king. As a result, the people escaped and gained a land of their own.

The laws showed people how to act as God did. God had sided with the poor; people ought to do the same.

The people often forgot that. Those who became rich and powerful ignored the humble start of their own nation. They were arrogant to the poor and made them suffer all the more.

It took a long time for the people to understand that God was not automatically on the side of their nation. Rather, God was on the side of what was right. Later, Old Testament writers suggested that many of the nation's disasters—defeat in war and so on—were the result of their failing to follow God's example and stand up for what was right and just.

God is love

From Old Testament times, people discovered that God's character never changed. Jesus taught that God's love is for everyone, including those whom no one else valued. He was always challenging those who were rich and powerful by the way He accepted people who had been mistreated and welcomed them to live as friends of God—to be part of what he called "God's kingdom."

At the end of the New Testament, the letters of John sum up the message of the entire Bible by saying "God is love."

7 The Book of God

What is God like?

All over the world, in all places and at all times, people have asked this question. It is not an easy one to answer. The question itself can mean many different things, such as "What does God look like?" "What is God made of?" or even "How does God behave?"

The Bible never tries to describe what God looks like or what God is made of. God is so different from everything else that answering these questions would be impossible.

Still, the Bible writers do believe that people can know something of God.

What or who is God?

In the Bible, people begin to answer this question by putting it the other way around, and saying what God is not:

▶ **God is not just the natural world.** The environment is very important and highly valued. But God is not the sky, or trees, or grass, or animals—or people.

▶ **God is not part of nature.** Some ancient people thought of their gods as things like fire, air, or water. These are all important for life, but in the Bible they are gifts that God gives to people, they are not gods themselves.

▶ **God is not a human person.** Many people have thought of gods as a kind of superrace, doing all the same things as women and men, but on a much grander scale. The Bible has a special place for people: They are "made in God's image." But God is different from people.

▶ **God is not a work of art.** Sometimes people have built statues and idols and worshiped them as gods. The Bible is quite clear that God is greater than anything people can make for themselves.

▶ **God is not an idea.** Christians have sometimes imagined that God must be the same as their own religious ideas. But the Bible's God is not that either.

The Bible says that people can never begin to understand all there is to know of God. God was in existence before everything else, and is the power at the root of everything—including human life.

▶ **God the party-giver**
Jesus told a story about God being like a king who gave a great feast. Some people felt they were too busy with other things to bother to go. But those who do put God first in their lives are welcome—including those who are often treated as unimportant: children, the poor, and disabled people.

Pictures of God

The Bible uses many word pictures to describe God. It takes things that its readers know about and says, "God is like this." God is compared to musical composers, gardeners, winemakers, women having children, shepherds, builders, hens, parents, dressmakers, and party-givers. God is also compared with natural features such as rocks.

▶ **God the rock**
In the Psalms God is described as being unshakable as a rock. With God, a person is safer than if they were in a strong fortress.

Speaking of God

God is neither male nor female. Because of the way some languages work, people have often spoken of God as "Him." The most helpful ways to speak of God are bound to vary in different times and places, and many Christians are no longer happy to speak as if God were a man.

▶ **God the mother bird**
The prophet Isaiah speaks of God as a mother bird—fierce and devoted in caring for her young.

Jesus

Christians believe that Jesus was God come to earth as a human. Jesus lived in a way that would show people what God is like. Christians claim that His teaching and example are at the center of the Bible's description of what God is really like. If anyone wants to know about God—look at Jesus.

8 Gods, Idols, and Images

It is not easy to worship an invisible God. Where does a person go to offer worship? What do they look at or think about?

The people of Israel believed in an invisible God, but they had made symbols of God's being with them. They built a temple in Jerusalem as a center for worship. Inside was the "ark of the covenant"—a golden box containing the tablets of stone with the Ten Commandments written on them. It was like an empty throne in a palace, reminding people of God's invisible presence.

The Ten Commandments clearly told people not to make idols, or bow down and worship them. There is a huge difference between a symbol and an idol.

A place for worship

When Solomon built the temple, he clearly understood that God did not actually "live" there, but he wanted a building that would help people worship.

Can you, O God, really live on earth? Not even all of heaven is large enough to hold you, so how can this Temple that I have built be large enough? LORD my God, I am your servant. Listen to my prayer, and grant the requests I make to you today. Watch over this Temple day and night, this place where you have chosen to be worshiped. Hear me when I face this Temple and pray. Hear my prayers and the prayers of your people when they face this place and pray. In your home in heaven hear us and forgive us.

▼ A symbol of God
The people of Israel made bulls to remind them of God's presence. They may have looked like this ancient bull statue.

Symbols and idols

A symbol is used to remind people of something important to them. Solomon's golden temple for God, built on a higher hill than his own palace, was a symbolic reminder that God was the true King of the people.

When Solomon died his kingdom was divided in two, and the temple in Jerusalem belonged only to the people in the southern kingdom of Judah. Jeroboam, the new king of the part known as Israel, built two new temples for his own people, at Bethel and Dan.

But there could only be one ark of the covenant, so Jeroboam needed something else to be a symbol of God's invisible presence. He had two golden bulls made instead. He intended them to be treated as symbolic thrones for a God who is invisible. But almost immediately, people started worshiping the bulls, as if they themselves were gods. The symbol was treated as an idol.

Gods of other nations

It was very hard for the people of Judah and Israel to be faithful to the laws God had given them.

▶ **Canaanite gods.** Long before the people of Israel set foot in the land of Canaan, where they made their home after they escaped from Egypt, other gods had been worshiped for centuries. And the Canaanites who worshiped them had certainly prospered; they had large cities and powerful armies and could grow good crops.

 The people of Israel knew their God could rescue slaves from Egypt, but they wondered if a God like that knew about life in cities and on farms? It seemed sensible to pay some attention to the Canaanite gods who were said to know about such things. Many people worshiped them alongside their own God.

▶ **Gods of Assyria and Babylon.** Israel and Judah were eventually both overrun by superpowers to the north—first Assyria and then Babylon. The rulers of these big empires did not want to take over everything, but they did expect conquered nations to pay regular taxes and do all they could to show they recognized who was in charge.

 Nowadays, a country might show it accepts being ruled by another by agreeing to have a new design of money, or speaking a different language. In ancient times, it meant putting up statues of foreign gods. For the sake of peace, some kings did exactly that—but they were strongly condemned by prophets who told them they were disobeying God's laws.

Controlling the gods

People are afraid of the mysterious forces in the universe. Making idols can be one way of bringing the gods down to size, in the belief they can then be controlled and kept happy.

▶ **Baal**
The Canaanites made idols of their gods, including the weather god, Baal.

Foreign gods: dead end or starting point?

Making idols of gods is always strongly condemned in the Old Testament, where it is seen as letting something else be more important than God. This approach to life is seen as a dead end—the wrong way to go.

 Centuries later, a Christian named Paul arrived in the Greek city of Athens and saw a Greek altar in honor of "the unknown god." Instead of disapproving of it, Paul made this his starting point. He spoke about the unknown god as a way of introducing Jesus, whom he believed had made God known to people in a new way.

9 Angels

Is there anything beyond the here and now?

It is a question that has fascinated people throughout the ages.

The ancient Greeks believed there is a spiritual world beyond this one, and life here is just a preparation for that. This world is second best, they thought, and the famous Greek philosopher Plato even wrote of the human body as a "prison" for the real person, which he believed was the "soul."

The Bible writers had no time for such ideas. The life of this world is good, they said, and people are here to make something beautiful out of it. That is why Bible stories are always about ordinary people and everyday life.

Angels

The word *angel* comes from a Greek word meaning "messenger," and in Bible stories angels do two things: They bring messages from God; and they help people, usually by keeping them safe from danger or encouraging or warning them in times of particular need.

In the Bible, angels often look just like ordinary people. It is only their extraordinary deeds that mark them as special:

▶ Abraham's nephew, Lot, lived in the city of Sodom. Two men came looking for lodgings, and Lot took them home. That night, a mob attacked him. The visitors rescued him and warned that the city was about to be destroyed. Lot followed their advice. When the city was burned he knew the visitors must have been angels.

An invisible other-world

The Bible writers did believe in the existence of another invisible world. But it was not a spirit world to which people would escape at death. It was the world where God is. They believed it could touch the lives of people in this world. Angels were one of the contact points.

Angel names

Beliefs about angels developed over a long period of time. By the time of Jesus, some angels were given personal names. The names of Gabriel and Michael are mentioned in the Bible, but there were also Uriel, Raphael, Raguel, Sariel, and Remiel.

▶ Once, a farmer named Gideon was harvesting wheat when a stranger suggested he lead his people against the Midianite raiders who were making life dangerous and difficult for them. When a meal mysteriously caught fire as the visitor touched it, Gideon knew it was an angel, and the message was from God.

▶ Elizabeth was an old woman, and she and her husband, Zechariah—who was a priest—had no children. One day as Zechariah was in the temple, an angel came and told him he and his wife would have a son. He didn't know what to say—in fact he remained speechless until the day his son was born. The son had a special message: to tell people of the coming of Jesus. He is known in the Bible as John the Baptist.

◀ **A shining angel**
Daniel describes a meeting with an angel dressed in a linen tunic, with a gold belt. The angel seemed to shine —like jewels, lightning, fire, and bronze.
And the angel said: "God loves you, so don't let anything worry you or frighten you."

Guardian angels

The New Testament includes references to guardian angels: They look after people by preserving them from danger, as well as staying close by at death.

Angels stood by Jesus when He was alone in the desert, and was tempted to give up the work of telling people about God even before He had begun.

Later, angels came to Him when He was praying in the Garden of Gethsemane, just a little while before His enemies arrested Him and had Him crucified.

Jesus Himself spoke of children having angels who looked after them and were concerned to protect them from losing their faith in God.

A warning
The New Testament book called Hebrews warns people not to let anything be more important to them than trust in God and Jesus. They must not begin to worship angels.

What are the angels, then? They are spirits who serve God and are sent by him to help those who are to receive salvation.

10 The Powers of Darkness

The Bible describes a God who made a good world, where people could love one another and have a happy life. But God never forces people to be good. They are free to decide for themselves how to live—and sometimes they make choices that are selfish and cruel. They hurt other people and damage the environment.

But why? When the Bible writers tackle this difficult question, they often use picture language. They call to mind a range of different ideas:

▶ **Sin.** This word is often used to describe wrongdoing—something people do even though they know it is against God's laws.

▶ **Fallen.** The Bible speaks of the world and its people as "fallen." This is a way of saying that everything and everyone are less than they should be; they suffer as a result of sin. So sin is more than just things that people do; it affects the world of nature as well.

▶ **Powers.** In some places, the Bible mentions powers that are working against God. Occasionally they are referred to as "demons," as if they were personal beings. More often, the term used is "principalities and powers." This can mean the unfair ways of organizing society so some people are always getting a raw deal.

Is there a devil?

The Bible is not about evil, but about goodness and God. This is God's world, it says, and it was made to be a safe place for people to become the best they can possibly be. At times of great sadness, it may seem as if God is no longer there. But the Bible never accepts that this world is in the control of evil powers.

So if there is a devil—some kind of chief evil power—it has a lot less power than God.

There are different opinions as to whether the Bible says there is a person or thing called the devil:

▲ **A fallen world**
The Bible says that God's good world is spoiled as a result of sin. Here, human greed for land has led to the destruction of great forests.

▶ **Victims of the rich and powerful**
The mention of evil powers in the Bible may refer to wrong ways of organizing society that leave some very rich and others very poor

- Poets often use words as symbols. These words put the reader in mind of something, but they are not meant to be taken literally, as they would be in a book of science. It may be that the word pictures used in the Bible to describe the effects of evil are symbolic. Some Bible writers describe evil as if it is a person, because that is something people can easily understand. It is worth remembering that they also describe God as a person sometimes, so people can glimpse what God is like. But they do not believe God actually has hands or ears or eyes or that the devil has horns.

- Others believe the Bible does intend to say there is a real devil. They look at things like the Nazi Holocaust, in which millions of Jewish people were murdered on the orders of Hitler, and they think the only possible explanation is that there must be a devil who was behind it all. Could anybody be as evil as Hitler was without being possessed by some force from outside himself?

Whatever the answer to that question, the Bible emphasizes that evil is very real, and its power has terrible effects in people's lives when they choose to follow it rather than staying faithful to God's laws.

▼ **The devil and the Holocaust**
In the Nazi Holocaust millions of Jews were put to death. Some people believe there must have been a devil behind this terrible event.

Children of different fathers

The writer of the letter of John speaks of God and the devil as fathers—there are people who have the family likeness of one, and others who have the family likeness of the other.

> *Whoever is a child of God does not continue to sin, for God's very nature is in him; and because God is his Father, he cannot continue to sin. Here is the clear difference between God's children and the Devil's children: anyone who does not do what is right or does not love his brother is not God's child.*

◄ **Dark of night**
It can be scary to be alone at night. The dark of night is often used in the Bible as a picture of what it feels like to be at the mercy of all kinds of evil things.

11 Magic and Miracles

The word *miracle* is often used to describe a happening that brings both amazement and delight. People use the word for different types of events.

▶ **Dreams come true.** Sometimes the good things of life seem out of reach. When they happen—when a person gets the chance they deserve, or when they win a prize—they may say "It's a miracle." In fact, *someone* had to be the winner.

▶ **Stunning science.** Think of someone from a remote tribe seeing a television for the first time. They might call it a miracle. Other people know it works in a straightforward scientific way, even if they can't explain it in detail.

▶ **Happenings beyond the ordinary.** Other "miracles" are events that seem to go against what people know of the way the world works. Sometimes a scientific explanation is eventually found. Other things continue to be impossible to explain.

Magic

Most Bible miracles just "happen." It seems that no extravagant ceremonies are needed before God acts. Magic is also described in the Bible: It is when people try to corner God into doing what they want. The Bible describes an event when worshipers of other gods, the prophets of Baal, shouted out and cut themselves to try to make their gods do what they wanted. But their magic ceremonies didn't work.

The Bible says that God cannot be blackmailed like that. Trying to work magic is forbidden. God does listen to people's prayers and wants the best for them. But God remains in charge.

Miracles in the Bible

Bible writers hardly ever use the word *miracle*. They just report events as they believed them to have happened, and accept that there are many things about the world no one can understand or explain. If this is God's world, they reason, then God is in charge of what happens, however surprising it might seem.

These surprising things fall into three main groups.

▶ **Nature miracles.** In quite a number of Bible stories, unexpected happenings in the world of nature changed people's lives. As Moses led the Israelite slaves from Egypt, they reached a shallow sea where reeds grew thickly. They crossed over when a strong wind blew the water to one side.

Later on in their adventures, a landslide blocked the river Jordan and allowed them to cross to the strong Canaanite city of Jericho.

Any of these events could have happened naturally. But it is certainly a miracle that they happened *when* they did. People saw God at work in the timing of these events.

▲ **Miraculous crossing**
The story of the Israelites' escape from Egypt says that God sent a wind to blow a path across the sea. The sea may have been a marshy area, with clumps of reed mace growing out of shallow water.

► **Healings.** The Bible tells many stories of people who were healed. A Syrian army officer, Naaman, bathed in the waters of the river Jordan on the instruction of the prophet Elisha, and a terrible skin complaint just disappeared.

Jesus anointed a blind man's eyes with mud, and he saw again.

One of the first Christians, Paul, let cloths he had used be taken to people who were ill, and they were healed.

► **Demons.** In ancient times, people often thought disease was the result of people doing wrong, or being possessed by demons. Somehow, evil had gotten into them.

The Bible teaches that sadness and suffering are part of the "fallen" state of this world (see page 10), not that illness is caused by the wrong things that individual people have done.

Casting out demons was one way of saying that this is God's world, and God's will is for people to be well in every respect—"whole." Jesus made many people "whole" in this way, enabling them to live life to the fullest.

Jesus and miracles

Jesus worked many miracles—stories describe Him calming a storm, healing people, raising dead people to life, casting out demons, and more.

Christians see Jesus' miracles as a sign that He really was God's special Messiah or Christ—sent to rescue the world from the powers of darkness and enable people to live life to the fullest, as God intended.

Did you know?

Christians see God at work whenever healing takes place. Often this is through the work of doctors using a range of medicines and other treatments. Other times a "miraculous" healing might take place.

▼ **Happy family**
Jesus brought happiness back to the family of a man named Jairus when he restored their twelve-year-old daughter to life again.

12 Dreams and Visions

People have always been fascinated by dreams and their meanings. In ancient Egypt and Babylon some people made a full-time job out of telling people what their dreams meant. They wrote books about how to understand dreams—some of which have been discovered and can still be read today!

People in Israel had less interest in this sort of thing, but they still believed that dreams and visions were important ways in which God could speak to people.

Visions

Visions are like vivid pictures that form in the mind, and they can happen at any time.

▶ **Some visions begin in real life.** The prophet Jeremiah saw a potter at work, and recognized this as a picture of what God is like, molding and making people. Amos saw a swarm of locusts eating everything in sight, and knew that the Assyrians would destroy the nation of Israel. When Isaiah saw the smoke and the fire on the altar in the temple, he knew God was speaking to him.

▲ **A vision of destruction**
Amos warned the people of Israel that the Assyrians would destroy their nation as a swarm of locusts lays land to waste.

▶ **Other visions come in a trance.** A person in a trance is awake, but their mind is so busy with one thing that they are not fully aware of all the everyday things going on around them. Peter had just completed saying prayers at midday when he fell into a trance: He saw something like a sheet being lowered down. On it were the kinds of animals Jews would never eat— but a voice was telling him to eat! Peter believed God was telling him to take the Christian message to people other than the Jews.

▶ **Visions as a secret language.** The messages of the books of Daniel and Revelation were both received in visions. They were written in secret coded language, and describe fierce battles between terrible monsters and dragons. Those who understood the code got the message: Though the forces of evil seemed very powerful, God was still in control of things.

▶ **Out-of-body experiences.** The Bible tells of some people who seemed to travel through time and space to far-off places. The prophet Ezekiel was living in Babylon, but he was taken hundreds of miles to see what was going on in Jerusalem. The apostle Paul wrote about an experience in which he was caught up to what he called "the third heaven" and had an especially close encounter with God.

The Bible writers had no doubt these things were all real. But what interested them most was not the experiences themselves but learning what God might be saying to them in this way.

Dreams

Dreams happen during sleep. In many stories, angels appeared to people in their dreams. As Jacob slept in the open air, he saw thousands of angels climbing up and down a ladder into the sky. Centuries later, Joseph learned in a dream that his fiancée, Mary, was to be the mother of Jesus.

This doesn't mean that every dream a person remembers is a message from God!

Christians might explain it like this: There are some things that come into their head—be they dreams or daytime thoughts—that seem to stay with them and just won't go away! Sometimes, as they turn the thing over in their mind, wondering why it seems so important, they become more and more convinced that these "loud" thoughts or "loud" dreams are a special message to them from God. What they read in the Bible and what Christian friends say about the thought or dream helps them figure out if this is the case.

Knowing what God wants

People in many different cultures have tried to find a way to discover what their god wants.

In Babylon, the priests of the Babylonian gods would cut open animals that had been killed as part of religious ceremonies. The way the insides looked was "read" as a kind of code.

The high priests of Israel's God kept two special tiles in a pocket in their ceremonial dress—the *Urim* and *Thummim*. One side meant yes and the other side meant no. When they needed to decide hard questions the high priests would throw them like dice to help them understand God's will.

◀ **Four horsemen**
The book of Revelation includes a terrifying vision of the forces of evil in the form of four horsemen and their riders. The rider of the white horse is a conqueror; the red a bringer of war; the black injustice; the pale horse, death.

Did you know?

The Bible makes it clear that unusual experiences are just one way that God communicates to people. The apostle Paul, in one of his letters to new Christians, said that they would know when they were doing as God wanted because they would feel a sense of inner peace. He wrote:

The peace that Christ gives is to guide you in the decisions you make.

13 Communicating with God

Prayer is the word used to describe communication with God. It includes listening to God and telling God things.

People at prayer

Communicating with God seems such a wonderful thing to do that it is hardly surprising that some people believe only special people can do it, perhaps in a special building, using special words.

According to the Bible, anyone can pray: God takes a personal interest in the lives of ordinary people and hears their prayers no matter where they are. Moses prayed on a mountain. Samuel prayed in bed. Miriam prayed in the middle of a long journey. Nehemiah prayed while serving wine to the emperor. Mary prayed in her relative's house when she was there on a visit. Paul prayed in prison. Jesus prayed in a garden.

Jewish people began and ended every day with a time of prayer. This was a useful reminder that God was there with them in both the daytime and the nighttime, but they knew God was with them always and people can pray at any other time, too.

Prayers can be long or short, said aloud or said silently. The person praying may make them up just as people do when talking to other people; or they may use the words of a prayer someone else has written. Some things people want to tell God are too hard to put into words—but the Bible says God understands sobbing and sighing just as well.

Christians make their prayers "in the name of Jesus," because they believe He is always speaking to God on their behalf.

When people set aside a special time and place for prayer, they sometimes choose a special posture to help them concentrate. In Bible times, people usually stood up to pray, with their hands lifted high. Sometimes they knelt, or lay facedown on the ground.

▶ A child prays
Anyone can pray. The boy Samuel prayed to God as he sat in his bed in the dark of night. Centuries later, Jesus said that one of the best places to pray was in a quiet room, alone.

◀ Arms outstretched
Early paintings of Christians at prayer show them with their arms outstretched. According to one writer, this was to remember Jesus, whose arms were held out on the cross.

Prayers from the Psalms

The psalms of the Bible include prayers that were used in worship.

- **Prayers of praise.** Praise the LORD, my soul! All my being praise his holy name.

- **Prayers of thanks.** I thank you, LORD, with all my heart.

- **Prayers for forgiveness.** Create a pure heart in me, O God, and put a new and loyal spirit in me.

- **Prayers for help.** When I am in trouble, don't turn away from me! Listen to me, and answer me quickly when I call!

The prayer Jesus taught

Jesus gave His disciples a prayer they could say. It is the starting point for all the prayers a person might say to God.

▶ First, the person praying addresses God:
  Our Father in heaven.

▶ Next come three items praising God:
  May your holy name be honored; may your Kingdom come; may your will be done on earth as it is in heaven.

▶ Then come three requests:
  Give us today the food we need. Forgive us the wrongs we have done, as we forgive the wrongs that others have done to us. Do not bring us to hard testing, but keep us safe from the Evil One.

▶ Christians later added a blessing with which to end the prayer:
  For the kingdom, the power and the glory are yours, now and for ever.

Answers to prayer

The Bible tells of many ways in which God answers prayer, and Christians are confident that God still answers prayer. Here are just a few examples.

- **Action.** Hannah was a married woman who had been childless for years. She prayed that she would have a baby—and within a year bore a son, Samuel.

- **A clear message.** A group of Christians in the church at Antioch wanted to know what God wanted them to do. According to the Bible, God spoke through a prophet, telling them to give Paul and Barnabas the special job of spreading the Christian message in other places.

- **Confidence in God's way.** Jesus prayed to be allowed to escape arrest and crucifixion. But as He prayed, He knew that this was not God's way for Him, and at last was able to accept that.

To discover what someone is like you really have to meet them in person.

Christians believe that God was once born into this world, as the baby Jesus. The event took place in Palestine around 2,000 years ago.

The people who met Jesus believed that they saw what God is like in all He did and said.

What they remembered of the things He did and said has been written down in the four accounts of his life in the Christian Bible—the Gospels of Matthew, Mark, Luke, and John. People today believe they can discover what Jesus is like by reading them. And as they get to know Jesus, they can meet God.

A special birth

The Bible stories of Jesus' birth say He was not the son of a human father, but the Son of God. An angel announced the news to Mary, an unmarried teenager, telling her that she was going to be the mother of God's Son. An angel gave the same news to her fiancé, Joseph.

Jesus' mother is referred to as the "Virgin Mary" because she had not had sexual relations with a man in order to become pregnant. Jesus' true Father is God.

Many Christians believe this story is literally true. Other Christians wonder if the story simply uses picture language to emphasize that Jesus was really in tune with God in a way no one has ever been.

However, there is no doubt as to the message of the stories. God did not come into the world as a king or as some great military leader who would order people to do right. Instead, God became a child and showed that the way to God's kingdom, to be one of God's people, had nothing to do with being powerful or rich.

▶ **A first glimpse of God**
According to Luke's Gospel, angels from heaven told shepherds to go and see the newborn baby lying in a manger in Bethlehem—they said the baby was Christ, the Messiah.

Jesus' names

Jesus is referred to by a lot of different names and titles. Here are some of the most often used. They all say something about what Jesus' followers believe about Him.

● **Jesus.** The angel who told Mary she was going to bear God's Son also told her to call her baby Jesus. This was a form of the Hebrew name "Joshua," and it was a first name in common use. It means "rescuer," and was to be a sign that Jesus would rescue people from the wrongdoing that makes the world such an unhappy place.

● **Christ or Messiah.** Jesus' followers also began to talk about Him as "Christ." This name comes from a Greek word meaning "anointed." The Hebrew word *Messiah* meant the same thing. In giving Jesus this title, people were saying they believed He was the special leader promised by God in the Old Testament—the One who would enable people truly to live as God's people.

● **Lord.** This was another name used in the early church to talk of Jesus. The Greek for it is *kurios*. In the Greek translation of the Old Testament, the word *kurios* was the personal name of God. Roman emperors called themselves *kurios* when they claimed to be divine—like the gods. Christians believed that Jesus really and truly was God.

● **Immanuel.** This was an Old Testament name also used to refer to Jesus at His birth. It meant "God is with us"—and that was the most important thing the Christians wanted to say about Him.

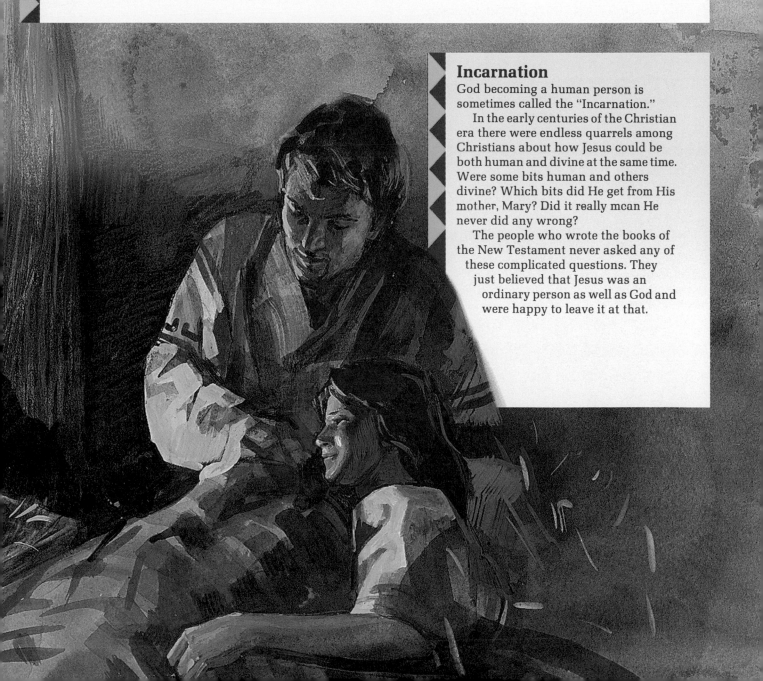

Incarnation

God becoming a human person is sometimes called the "Incarnation."

In the early centuries of the Christian era there were endless quarrels among Christians about how Jesus could be both human and divine at the same time. Were some bits human and others divine? Which bits did He get from His mother, Mary? Did it really mean He never did any wrong?

The people who wrote the books of the New Testament never asked any of these complicated questions. They just believed that Jesus was an ordinary person as well as God and were happy to leave it at that.

Jesus: Life and Death

Jesus grew up in a small town in Palestine called Nazareth. When He was about thirty, He gave up His work as a carpenter and builder and spent all His time telling people about God.

A message of life

Jesus said that anyone who wanted to be part of God's people had simply to turn to God as to a loving parent. They will discover how much God loves them. They will know real happiness and live life to the fullest—as God always intended people to.

Knowing lots of things about religion wasn't important. Anyone who wanted to be part of God's kingdom—God's people— was welcome, including little children. Indeed, children provided the very best example of how to come close to God! Having many good deeds to boast about was no use at all! No one could ever live a good enough life to match God's standards. People who had worked really hard to keep God's laws were no better than people who had messed up their lives with all kinds of wrong things. They both needed God's forgiveness, but with God's help they could live better lives.

▲ **Welcome in God's kingdom**
Jesus said that children were welcome in God's kingdom, and could enter it easiest of all. These children in a Mozambique Sunday school are praying.

FRIENDS WITH GOD

"One day," said Jesus, "two people went into the temple to pray. One of them was very religious. He knew all the right things to say and do for God. He took one look at the other person and began his prayer: 'O God, I'm so glad I'm not like him.' And he went on to tell God lots of great things about himself.

"The other man had no idea how to pray, and he knew only too well that his life was a mess. 'God,' he said. 'I've made many mistakes—and I know nothing about religion, but please hear me.'

"Now," asked Jesus, "which one went home friends with God?"

Everyone was amazed at the answer. "The second one," said Jesus. "Only he saw his need of God."

Condemned to death

Jesus was loved by many people for the good and kind things He did: helping them to turn their lives around, healing people who were sick, welcoming those who had no friends.

But He also made many enemies, including some of the religious leaders, who did not like the way He talked about God's love and forgiveness.

In the end, they told lies about Him to get Him into trouble with the Romans who ruled the land, and had Him put to death on a cross—crucified.

His followers were crushed. How could such a thing happen to the One they believed was God's Messiah? What had happened to His message of a full and happy life—safe with God forever?

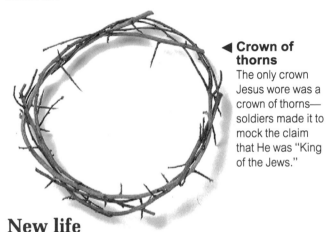

◄ Crown of thorns
The only crown Jesus wore was a crown of thorns—soldiers made it to mock the claim that He was "King of the Jews."

New life

Three days after Jesus was crucified and laid in a tomb, His followers began seeing Him alive again. They were utterly astonished. But they were also quite convinced that it was true.

As they thought about these amazing events, it all began to make sense, and became an important part of their beliefs.

Jesus had risen from the dead, so—

▶ they knew that Jesus really had overcome all the powers of evil in the world.

▶ they knew there must be something else after death.

▶ they looked forward to a time when everything would be made new, and those who followed Jesus would share in His glory.

Jesus' coming to life again is often called the Resurrection.

16 The Way Back to God

After Jesus rose from the dead (see page 15), Jesus' followers looked back over their Jewish faith, and began to understand it in a new way. One important question they looked at was how the faith had helped people build a relationship with God.

The great rift

The first story in the Bible told them that, from the beginning, people were made to be God's friends. Their wrongdoing ruined the relationship.

A way to worship

It was through worship that the people of Israel could come close to God again. In Old Testament times, there were many special offerings they should make to God.

These special offerings were called sacrifices. The people always offered to God their most valuable things—their crops and animals.

They brought the offerings to their special place of worship. In the early days this was a tent, the tabernacle. Hundreds of years later Solomon built the first temple in Jerusalem to replace it.

The place of worship had a stone altar, like a huge hearth, where some parts of the offering were burned. The rest provided food for the priests.

People offered crops as a way of giving thanks to God. But when animals were killed in sacrifice, they were a way of asking God's forgiveness for wrongdoing. It was as if the animals were suffering the fate the people deserved because of their sin.

▼ Altar
This stone altar has been built in the way described in the Old Testament. Sacrifices were burned on the flat top of an altar.

◄ Sheep
Sheep were among the animals commonly offered as sacrifices in worship.

Worship without a temple

In 586 B.C. the Babylonian emperor Nebuchadnezzar destroyed Solomon's grand temple in Jerusalem. Most of the people were forced to live in other countries. But they believed that the temple was the only place where it was right to offer sacrifices.

Instead, they built meeting places known as synagogues. Here, they worshiped God by saying prayers, reading the Scriptures, and talking together about what the Scriptures meant.

Synagogue and temple

Eventually the people who had been taken away to Babylon were allowed to return to Jerusalem to rebuild their homes and their temple.

By the time of Jesus, Herod the Great had built a magnificent temple in Jerusalem. People met in the synagogues each week and went to the temple when they were in Jerusalem, especially at festival times.

Jesus said that the time was coming when the place of worship simply wouldn't matter:

The time is coming and is already here, when by the power of God's Spirit people will worship the Father as he really is.

Christian worship

From the start of the church on the Day of Pentecost, Christians believed that God was with them in a special way—as the Holy Spirit.

God's laws still guided them, but no one could ever keep the law well enough to meet God's standards. New Christians were baptized—dipped in water—to show that by God's spirit they would be changed from the inside and would make a new start in life.

From now on they could worship God in a personal way. Christians needed no special buildings, they had no priests and they never offered any sacrifices.

However, in explaining what they believed about Jesus, they took ideas from Old Testament descriptions of worship.

Peter wrote that the Christians themselves were both temple and priests:

Come as living stones, and let yourselves be used in building the spiritual temple, where you will serve as holy priests to offer spiritual and acceptable sacrifices to God through Jesus Christ.

He also described Jesus' death on the cross as a sacrifice, which had put right all the wrong that was in the world.

Christians remembered the time just before Jesus died when He had shared bread and wine with His close friends. He had said then that He was going to die for them, and that they must continue to share bread and wine to remember that fact.

Sharing bread and wine became a very important part of their worship.

Did you know?
John the Baptist called Jesus the "lamb of God ... who takes away the sin of the world." It is a name that reminds people of the belief that Jesus was the final sacrifice, provided by God.

◄ Sharing bread and wine
From the earliest days of Christianity, the followers of Jesus shared bread and wine as Jesus had told them to. It was to remember that Jesus had died for them so they could have a way back to God.

The Holy Spirit

The very first page of the Bible describes how God is involved in what goes on in this world and is concerned for the lives of ordinary people.

But how can God be God and still be part of everyday life? One way the Bible answers that question is by speaking of God's Spirit. Once again, this is picture language. In the Bible other things are used to help describe the Holy Spirit. The two most commonly used are wind and a dove.

▼ Former enemies
Christians believe it is the Holy Spirit that changes them and enables them to show love to one another. Former enemies are able to accept one another.

In the early church, this included Greeks and Jews, soldiers and tax collectors, slaves and slave owners, men, women, and children.

This picture shows an incident told in the New Testament, in which a wealthy man named Philemon welcomes back a runaway slave, Onesimus, as a fellow Christian.

◄ Wind
Wind blowing over water is a reminder of God's Spirit at creation.

God's Spirit at creation

The book of Genesis begins by telling how the world came into being as God's Spirit blew over the watery chaos that was there before anything came into existence. It is a way of saying that nothing happens without God being involved.

God's Spirit and the prophets

The Old Testament often says that when prophets received God's message, these were sent by God's Spirit.

God's Spirit in Jesus

The Bible says that Jesus' birth came about through the work of God's Spirit. When Jesus was baptized to mark the beginning of His teaching work, John the Baptist said he saw the Spirit hovering over Him like a dove. Later, Christians said that Jesus' resurrection was the work of God's Spirit. Throughout, they believed that God was at work in Jesus' life and teaching in a unique way.

God's Spirit in Christians

Some of the Old Testament prophets had hoped for a time when everyone in the whole world would live so close to God that they could be described as "filled with the Spirit."

The early Christians believed this had happened to them as a result of Jesus' death and resurrection. As they followed Jesus, they found their lives were transformed. They were just ordinary people, but they could do extraordinary things with God's help.

Some of these things were—and are—quite spectacular. For example, some were given special ability to heal people. Others were able to give people messages from God—prophecy.

But the most extraordinary thing that happens to ordinary followers, says the Bible, is that God gives them a new nature. Instead of following human nature, which goes its own selfish way, they long to live as God's friends. God's Spirit helps people live and to do what is right:

The Spirit produces love, joy, peace, patience, kindness, goodness, faithfulness, humility, and self-control.

God's Spirit and the Bible

The Bible used by the first Christians was a Greek translation of the Hebrew Scriptures, called the Septuagint. The New Testament speaks of these writings being inspired by God's Spirit.

Later, when the books of the New Testament had been gathered together, they, too, were believed to have been inspired in the same way. All these books were written by ordinary people, but they revealed many things about God.

God: Finding the Right Description

Christians believe that God is so different from anything in this world that ordinary words can never be enough.

As a result, the Bible always uses picture language for God. These pictures describe God as being like something that people can easily understand (page 10).

In the early years of the church, Christians began using three words more than others to describe God: *Father, Son,* and *Holy Spirit.* These three together are known as the "Trinity."

Trinity

In several of the New Testament books, the three ways of describing God are found together, as part of a blessing: "The grace of the Lord Jesus Christ, the love of God, and the presence of the Holy Spirit be with you all." They sum up three important things about God's character.

The Bible writers used many other picture words to describe God, but these three became the most important.

Did you know?
God is described as Father, Son, and Holy Spirit together several times in the New Testament—but the Bible never once uses the word *Trinity.*

It is a word that Christians have chosen since to express a very hard idea—that there is one God who is at work in many different ways.

▼ The Son's message
Jesus' invitation to those who wanted to live as God's friends was simple: "Follow me." Everything He said and did was an example of how they should live—loving God and other people.

▲ The Father's world
Christians believe that this world is God's creation.

▶ God the "Father" means God as the Creator of all things, the One who cares for the whole world, its plants, animals, and people. According to the Bible God made a good world, where people could live at peace with the natural world and with one another.

▶ **God the "Son"** refers to God as the One whose love is known through Jesus, who came to mend the friendship between God and people.

▶ **God the "Spirit"** means God as the One who is always at work changing things for the better, transforming all that there is.

▲ **The power of the Spirit**
Birds wheel and soar on invisible air currents. The power of air to lift things is a picture of God's Spirit, which is unseen yet powerful to bring change.

19 What Happens After Death?

▲ **Ready for the afterlife**
The Egyptians provided their dead with things they believed they would need for an afterlife.

What happens after death? It is a question that just about everyone asks—for everyone has to die.

The books of the Bible were written over a period of a thousand years, and in that time, people's beliefs changed.

Death and the Old Testament

In Old Testament times, some nations believed there was life after death inside the grave—or in a place people could only reach through the grave. Egyptians filled the pyramids with furniture and food so those who were entombed there would have enough to last them in their future life. Canaanite tombs had chutes through which people could send food and drink to their dead relatives. They feared the dead could affect the living: If they were happy and well fed they would use their influence for good rather than evil.

The people of Israel were influenced by the nations around them, but had their own beliefs.

▶ **Letting the dead be.** King Saul seems to have shared something of the Canaanite belief that the dead could use their influence to help the living. He asked a Canaanite woman to help him get in touch with the dead prophet Samuel for this reason. But he was condemned for it: The Old Testament message is that people should depend on God, not on the dead.

▶ **Children.** Most Old Testament books assume that after they die, people and their influence live on through their children. That is one reason why people so much wanted to have children—and had sympathy for those who were unable to do so.

▶ **Sheol.** Some passages speak of the dead continuing to live on in a place called Sheol. The Bible never says much about what kind of place this might be. It is shadowy, quite unlike later ideas about heaven and hell. But God knows what is going on there.

▶ **Justice at last.** By the very end of Old Testament times, people were developing a clearer view of life after death. The book of Daniel says that there will be justice in the end for good people who suffer unfairly.

New Testament times

In the time of Jesus, many Jewish people believed in life after death. Those who lived good lives would rise again to receive their rewards, and those who had been evil would be punished.

▶ **Pharisees.** One group of people called Pharisees included many experts in God's law. The Pharisees believed the law could be understood in new ways for new situations, and they believed in life after death.

▶ **Sadducees.** Another group of people were called the Sadducees. Most of them were aristocrats and priests. They refused to believe anything that could not be found in the law books of the Old Testament.

Before becoming a Christian, the missionary Paul had been a Pharisee. When his enemies took him to court for his beliefs in Jesus, he noticed that some of the judges were Pharisees and the rest Sadducees. He told them he was still a good Pharisee because he believed in a future life. Instead of dealing with him, the court officials started arguing among themselves.

▶ **Christians.** The Christians always believed in life after death, because they were sure of their belief that Jesus was alive again after His crucifixion. That gave them the confidence to know that death was not the end, but the start of a new experience of life in the presence of God.

◀ **Seed and plants**
A buried seed becomes a wonderful new plant. This everyday event provides a glimpse of how Christians believe people will be raised to new life.

Body and soul

The Greeks thought people consisted of bodies and souls, and the soul lived on after the body was dead. The Hebrew people saw things differently. Even when they came to believe in life after death, they always spoke of the whole person being raised, not just a "soul."

The person would have a new kind of body, right for the new life. Paul wrote this to new Christians in the Greek town of Corinth:

Someone will ask, "How can the dead be raised to life? What kind of body will they have?"

You fool! When you plant a seed in the ground, it does not sprout to life unless it dies. And what you plant is a bare seed, perhaps a grain of wheat.... God provides that seed with the body he wishes; he gives each seed its own proper body.... When buried, it is ugly and weak; when raised, it will be beautiful and strong.

20 A Lasting Hope

The Bible's stories describe life as it really is—the bad times as well as the good. Its first stories set the scene: a world God made good, spoiled by wrongdoing.

The Bible and real life

The world of the Bible has much in common with everyday life in every age. True, it was written a long time ago, and the way of life of its people is often quite different. But people are always people and the problems they face are very similar to those people face today.

▶ **Family life.** The people in Abraham's family had a really hard time. He let them down, told lies, and was violent. But knowing God made a difference. Abraham was challenged to change, and his wives and children found new strength to cope.

　　The prophet Hosea thought he had a happy home, but then his wife fell in love with someone else. She ended up as a prostitute, and was forced to sell herself as a slave in the marketplace. When Hosea saw her, he knew he still loved her. God gave him the courage to take her home and care for her.

▶ **Crushing disappointments.** Sometimes a person feels that everything is going wrong for them. In the Bible story, a man named Job lost everything unfairly. The writer of a book called Ecclesiastes was unsure whether life could ever be happy. There were times when even God seemed hostile and hard to understand.

▶ **National disaster.** Sometimes a country or a nation seems to suffer more than is fair. In the Bible, the people of Israel knew God's protection when they escaped from slavery in Egypt. But it was hard to make their home in the new land, and even harder to be loyal to God when the Canaanites seemed to be doing so well following other gods. The people of Israel were defeated by the Assyrians and the Babylonians, and were never really free after that. Yet the Bible writers were sure that God was with them.

▼ **Bitter realities**
The world can be a bitterly cruel and unjust place—as for this woman, begging for money so she can buy a simple funeral for a dead relative. Christians believe that Jesus brings hope in times like these.

Jesus brings hope

The first Christians believed it was worth trusting God because of what they saw in Jesus. Jesus himself knew what it was like to live and die in this world. He knew what it was like to feel that God had left Him to suffer alone on the cross. He said aloud a prayer He remembered from the Psalms: *My God, my God, why have you abandoned me?*

But the Resurrection gave them hope that could not be crushed. God was there through all the suffering. And God would put everything right in the end.

▼ Pearly gates

On the last page of the Bible, the writer of Revelation talks of being taken by an angel to look down on the holy city of God—built of gold and jewels, with gates of pearl, and lit by the light of God.

Heaven and hell

Jesus once told a story about two men who died on the same day. One was very rich. The other was very poor. In fact, he was a beggar outside the rich man's gate.

When they died, the poor man went to heaven where he enjoyed all the comforts he had been denied. The rich man went to a place called "Hades" where he was punished for his selfishness.

Bible descriptions of Hades, or hell, were based on a garbage pit called Gehenna, just outside Jerusalem, where rubbish was continually burning day and night.

By the Middle Ages, artists were drawing detailed paintings of life in heaven and hell, and religious people put quite a lot of effort into imagining what went on there.

The Bible makes it plain that at the end of time all the wrongs in the world will be put right. But experts are unsure whether its descriptions of heaven and hell are meant to be taken literally, or whether they are part of the picture language that is used all the time to describe the work of God.

A new heaven and a new earth

The last book of the Bible, Revelation, speaks with great confidence of the future. It was written at a time when Christians were suffering a great deal for their faith, but it is full of hope.

The writer is clearly quite certain that Jesus did rise from the dead, and that God will put right all the wrongs in the world. There will be justice at last:

At the end of time, there will be a new heaven and earth. People will live in the holy city of God. God will be there, and will wipe the tears from eyes that cry. There will be no more death, sadness, crying or pain.

Finding Out More

If you want to know more about what you've read in *Amazing Bible Mysteries*, you can look up the stories in the Bible.

The usual shorthand method has been used to refer to Bible passages. Each Bible book is split into chapters and verses. Take **1 Kings 17:19–22**, for example. This refers to 1 Kings; chapter 17; verses 19–22.

When a reference to a Gospel story has other references after it in brackets, this means that the same story has been told by more than one of the Gospel writers.

1   History and Mystery

Judges 6:11; 1 Kings 17:19–22; Jonah 1:11–15; Matthew 4:1 (Mark 1:12; Luke 4:1); Mark 7:32–35; Acts 16:16	**History and Mystery**
Isaiah 36:1–2	**History in the making**

2   A Slice of Life

Matthew 12:9–14 (Mark 3:1–6; Luke 6:6–11)	**Synagogue ruins**
Psalm 119:105	**Ancient lamp**
Jeremiah 19:1–11	**Potted history**
Mark 14:13–15 (Luke 22:8–12)	**Old Testament jugs**
Matthew 3:11 (Mark 1:7; Luke 3:16; John 1:26–27)	**Sandals**

3   Landmark Events

Daniel 9:1	**Written details**
Isaiah 36:1–2	**The Judean story**

5   Mysteries Beyond Time

Genesis 1:27–30; Exodus 34:6–7; Micah 6:8	**Another story**

6   A God of Love and Justice

Genesis 1:1–24	**A life-giving God**
Exodus 13:7–14, 22:21–22, Leviticus 19:9–10; Isaiah 58:1–7; Jeremiah 32:16–32	**A God of justice**
Hosea 11:1–9; Luke 15:8–10; John 4:1–26; 1 John 4:7	**God is love**

7   The Book of God

Genesis 3:21; Psalm 18:2, 40:3; Isaiah 5:1–7, 42:14; Hosea 11:1; Matthew 22:1–10, 23:37; Luke 13:34, 14:15–24; John 10:11; Hebrews 11:10; Revelation 22:1	**Pictures of God**
Matthew 22:1–10 (Luke 14:15–24)	**God the party-giver**
Psalm 18:2	**God the rock**
Exodus 19:4	**God the mother bird**

8   Gods, Idols, and Images

1 Kings 8:27–30	**A place for worship**
1 Kings 12:1–17, 25–30	**Symbols and idols**
1 Kings 18:1–40	**Canaanite gods**
2 Kings 17:21–23; 25:8–12	**Gods of Assyria and Babylon**
2 Kings 17:13–18; Acts 17:16–31	**Foreign gods: dead end or starting point?**

9   Angels

Genesis 19:1–29; Judges 6:11–24; Luke 1:5–25, 57–66	**Angels**
Daniel 10:12–14; Luke 1:26	**Angel names**
Daniel 10:4–19	**A shining angel**
Matthew 4:11 (Mark 1:12–13); 18:10; Luke 22:43; Acts 27:23–24	**Guardian angels**
Hebrews 1:14	**A warning**

10   The Powers of Darkness

Matthew 8:28–34 (Mark 5:1–20; Luke 8:26–39); Romans 3:23, 8:19–21; Ephesians 6:12	**The Powers of Darkness**
Psalm 22:1; John 16:31–33 Romans 5:12	**Is there a devil?**
1 John 3:9–10	**Children of different fathers**
John 13:30	**Dark of night**

11   Magic and Miracles

Exodus 14:21–22; Joshua 2:14–17	**Nature miracles**
1 Kings 18:20–29	**Magic**
Exodus 14:21–22	**Miraculous crossing**
2 Kings 5:1–19; John 9:1–7; Acts 19:12	**Healings**
Matthew 17:14–18 (Mark 9:14–27; Luke 9:37–43); John 9:1–3	**Demons**
John 20:30–31	**Jesus and miracles**

Index